Breath of Life

Breath of Life

A MEMOIR

Mia

BREATH OF LIFE
A MEMOIR

iUniverse books may be ordered through booksellers or by contacting:

iUniverse
1663 Liberty Drive
Bloomington, IN 47403
www.iuniverse.com
1-800-Authors (1-800-288-4677)

ISBN: 978-1-4917-6379-7 (sc)
ISBN: 978-1-4917-6381-0 (hc)
ISBN: 978-1-4917-6380-3 (e)

Library of Congress Control Number: 2015905895

Print information available on the last page.

iUniverse rev. date: 06/09/2015

Table of Contents

For my Grandpa and
my Mother

In memory of Shantel,
and those who took their own lives too soon

Acknowledgements

To my one and only son - thank you for giving me so much to laugh about despite all I've been through. You are the reason I've persevered through it all.

To the friends who have read my manuscript, supported my efforts and encouraged me on this journey.

To my Savior, my God, my King. Thank you for the gift of salvation and the peace and healing you have blessed me with.

Introduction

We all have a story. Pain, fear, anger and at times, depression, grip all our lives. My story is no different. I simply choose to share this journey with you. Why, you may ask? Well, because my life experience has included so much pain, I don't want someone else to go through the same. As you read my story, you will find I have shared raw emotion at the twists and turns that life has shown me. It is no understatement to say I am fortunate, by the grace of God, to have survived. I know this is true.

Ultimately, I hope to inspire you in your faith and in the belief that life is good, even when you can see no purpose for all you may have had to endure. To inspire courage - that being honest about ourselves and our own shortcomings, is not really a weakness but rather, a strength in our own cognizance. I've often said that "I'm not a surface dweller." Do I want to look nice on the outside? Of course I do! But I want my inside to be whole, happy, cared for and beautiful as well. And in order for me to do that, I talk about my life's experience. I don't sweep it under the rug and try to hide from it. When you do that, a part of the memory will always control you. I can't live that way. So I write of this life, and hope and pray that someone, even if it's just one person, will benefit from my experience.

My hope for women especially, is that they will value their bodies, their sexuality and the creation of life in new and synergistic ways. Life is often about the choices we make at critical intersections. The story that follows is illustrative of how choice can have a negative impact on one's life, even when it may seem you have made the best decision at the time. And ultimately it's about forgiving oneself and coming to grips with the reality of life, that it is no fairytale….. Prince Charming is not knocking at the door, but that every day, there is something to be grateful for, even if it's just the breath of life.

Beginnings

October 1, 2001

Dear Lord,

Help me share this journey of mine,
so that from my pain, others may find freedom.
Let me share this journey from darkness
into the Kingdom of Light and Truth.
And in the process Lord, most importantly,
may Your name be praised
and Your Glory raised.

When I was a little girl, I was the queen of magical thinking. I wasn't aware that I was doing this at such a young age, but I used theophany (to make things seem God-like) to the nth degree.

I imagined that my family as a unit was "perfect" and I thought my parents were too. I'm not sure how I reached that conclusion since my dad seemed to drink a lot, but I had him on a pedestal along with everyone else: my mother, brother and sister.

Maybe I felt this way because my Dad would give me his undivided attention every once in awhile. He wasn't around much but when he was he would tickle me and call me "chuggy buggy" and make me feel special in a way that no one else in my family did. For as long as I can remember my Dad drove a Cadillac and he liked listening to his eight tracks in the car. One of the songs that was popular at the time was "Windy," by the Association. When that song was playing he would sing it out loud to me and replace Windy with my nickname - "Shelly."

It wasn't much, but in his own way, I thought my Dad loved me. Sometimes on the way home from the country club in the summers my Dad would stop for a drink at one of his favorite spots. I would get a Coca-Cola or sometimes, as a real treat, he would buy me a Shirley Temple. Maybe it was my Dad's job that led me to ignore his passion for scotch, or maybe it was just the fact that he paid attention to ME once in awhile! I don't know. The rest of my family paid very little attention to me whatsoever, but still I kept them on a pedestal. I was the youngest - I looked up to them all - like I thought I was supposed to.

My Dad was a golf pro - the head golf professional at a private country club. "The Club" had an 18-hole golf course, a swimming pool, clubhouse and banquet facilities and if there was a golf tournament or a wedding reception (or both), on any given weekend, the place would be packed with people. As a young girl I was fortunate to spend many hours of those precious summer days at the swimming pool. I was often one of the last people to leave. It was a haven for me, my safe place, without my even knowing it at the time. I loved the feeling within me, the soothing relaxation in my muscles, after a day of sunshine and being in the water.

I could practice diving or swimming and do whatever I wanted because most of the time it seemed like I was there by myself - hanging out with friends and their parents. When I was younger, my mom would come to the pool for the day and hang around with the other moms, but she didn't know how to swim, so I never saw her in the water much. There was a time when we were on vacation once in Florida when I was about three or four (before I could really swim) and she thought I was drowning and she jumped in the water to save me, so I know my mother loved me. It just wasn't reflected in my world enough that it seemed real to me.

My sister would come to the pool occasionally also, but she didn't seem to enjoy it the way I did. And my brother was never around. He was always working in the pro shop, cleaning clubs, caddying, or doing something related to golf. So I never saw him much either. I wasn't aware of it at the time consciously, but I know now that those days left me feeling relieved, yet lonely. Since I was the youngest and usually ignored by my older siblings, I guess I didn't mind. I was relieved that they weren't around, relieved from the additional emotional pain of being ignored - I had enough of that when we were all together. I didn't particularly care for being ignored either. It made me want to crawl inside myself and disappear. Little did I know, that those precious summers would become some of the very best times of my childhood, my most treasured memories.

Away from the pool and the club, we lived in a nice middle class neighborhood, in a small town about an hour west of Boston. Our neighborhood was filled with kids, who thankfully, were mostly MY age. That helped make up for the being ignored at home stuff. My best friend, Sandy, lived next door and we were the same age, born only twelve days apart. She was almost like a sister to me - we even looked alike in some ways. We both had brown hair, and were about the same size. Sandy's house was the 'hub' of Sierra Drive; everyone was always welcome and it was usually a busy place.

Whether it was Kick the Can, pickle, kick ball or softball, we always found something fun to do in the neighborhood. While we waited for the bus in the mornings, we would play jump rope. In the summers sometimes we would all have a camp out and sleep under the stars outside. A couple of the families had pools in their backyard so on the rare summer day when I didn't go to the club, I was still able to go swimming.

I remember these summers with great fondness because I was safe and happy, (so I thought) and as a child, life was pretty carefree. I didn't realize it then, but what I know now is that I could actually feel God's love and presence during those wonderful summer days, which is why I remember them better than anything else. But ever since I was six, my mother had been depressed and even hospitalized once for depression. I don't remember who took care of us or what happened, while she was gone. My only memory of this event, is waving to her from the parking lot as she stood in a window at the hospital. I don't remember asking anything about it, or anyone explaining why she was in the hospital. Nevertheless it remained tucked away in my mind.

As a child, Halloween was never my favorite holiday to celebrate because that meant you had to dress up in a costume - which would bring attention to yourself. I wasn't used to that. This particular year that my mother was hospitalized, she had bought me a princess costume for Halloween. Huh. It was the best costume she'd ever gotten me and for once, it did make me feel special, since my Dad had always called my sister "princess."

If summers held lots of fun, the winters matched up just as well with lots of activities. There was ice skating, hockey and plenty of sledding and snowball fights. There were times when we'd get a foot or two of snow and when the driveway was cleared, the piles would be higher than the car. We'd go to the end of the driveway and dig out the snow to build forts on each end so we could have a snow ball war. Of course, I was never any match for the bullets my brother would throw at me, but it was good practice for me to work on my throwing arm.

My throwing arm was pretty good, for a girl. I can remember playing third base and shortstop during my years in softball. Actually I played almost every position over the years, and usually with pretty good proficiency. In the early years I did a lot of pitching, because I was always pretty accurate. I liked second base and I didn't mind the outfield either. I liked catching fly balls. It kind of reminded me of shagging golf balls for my dad - although I didn't catch those, of course.

These are the positive, joyful memories of my childhood. Summer sunshine, drying out from a swim, diving, late afternoons with the sun setting on the golf course, or, warm mittens from the furnace that we would put on for the next round of sledding, ice skating or street hockey. Of course, few of us are fortunate to escape childhood without collecting unpleasant memories as well. That's just life. I can recall as a child feeling so rejected and unwanted that I would go and hide in a corner of the living room behind the couch and wait for someone to come find me, hoping that someone would notice and miss me. No one ever did. Gradually, as I began to realize that it seemed my participation in family conversation was not real welcome, and my presence was not missed, I told myself that no one cared or loved me. What a lie. But from the environment I was growing up in, this lie seemed very true at the time and I wasn't hearing anything differently through church. Because of my mother's own illness and struggle with depression, she was unable to get us to church or Sunday school on any regular basis. When my sister and I shared a room together (I was about eight or nine) she would tell me on Sunday mornings, "Shhhh, don't wake up Mom! I don't want to go to church." Of course, little sister obeyed, even though part of me didn't want to at all. I didn't mind going to church, I actually kind of liked it and enjoyed the peace I felt while I was there, but I was always trying to keep everyone else happy.

Eventually my sister took over the den downstairs when we remodeled the garage and turned it into a family room. We were no longer roommates, which was really to her disadvantage, although she might not have seen it that way. Now, her room was such a mess that there was no clear cut path to get from one side of the room to the other. You just kind of waded through the clothes and piles of stuff. I would get so bad that I'd clean it for her, without her even asking.

I thank God for my sister, Sherry, because if it weren't for her, my mother and I wouldn't have found quite as much to laugh at - because her and I were so much alike. Certain incidents still remain in my memory about the laughter we shared. One particular day that I'll never forget was when we were wallpapering the bathroom in the lower level after she'd moved downstairs. My mom had chosen a really cute black and white print and decided she wanted to do the ceiling as well. For some reason, this had become a three person project, and as my mother stood there holding up the paper on the ceiling, to know where to cut, my sister put her nose right under my mom's armpit and sniffed loudly! Needless to say all the wallpaper came falling down as my mother's arms did too. We all laughed so hard - she was just hilarious.

I was born the favorite, or so my siblings seemed to think. They probably felt that way because I was the youngest and my mother had given my middle name after my grandfather - Meredith. They had both been named by our father. My brother and sister used to try to convince me that I was adopted; at one point they were so successful, that my mother drove to the closest department store she could find to buy a baby book for me, because she'd never made one when I was born. That didn't redeem me or make much difference in my eyes. It seemed to me that a baby book should be something you filled out when the child was born, to mark the joyful occasion when it happened. No baby book just confirmed what I felt deep in my spirit at a young age: I was not really wanted.

Church as I remembered it, was at the Trinity Church in downtown Northbridge. We were Protestant - unlike most of my friends and their families, I remember that every Wednesday night my best friend Sandy, went off to catechism. I never had a clue what that was until I began my own spiritual journey later on in life. It seemed like everyone around us was Catholic or Episcopalian and I didn't know what that meant or what the difference was. I didn't even know that in Protestant denominations you became "confirmed" also, I thought that was for Catholics only. All I remember about church, for the most part, was the fear of fidgeting too much upstairs in "the big church" and my mother making life miserable for us if she deemed our behavior unacceptable. The church upstairs where the adults went was beautiful – with a deep red carpet and long rows of white pews, burgundy velvet padded seats and a wonderful organ. As a young girl I took piano lessons from the church organist and she even encouraged me to sing in the choir. I did sing once, but I was never encouraged to pursue it again - like so many of my other dreams. I wanted to be an Olympic swimmer, diver or ice skater. Although I participated in these activities, and was told I was good at them, for one reason or another - my future was never shaped around them.

So, the years rolled by and my childhood passed far too quickly. Those days of innocence and just being a kid were reluctantly replaced with more grown up things. I remember realizing in the fourth grade that one of the boys in my class had a crush on me. I didn't quite know what to think about that. During lunchtime at school, the boys would sometimes tear out the word "sweetheart" from the paper straw wrappers and pass them to me, but I don't recall ever trying to find out who they were from. The wonders of boy-girl relationships were a mystery to me and I didn't put a lot of time into thinking about them. I even stayed home from school on Valentine's Day that year out of embarrassment and fear. I didn't know what it all meant and my mother was not offering any insight into the mystery of it all (which was the same way she was raised).

Once I made it to junior high (sixth grade), I was so excited! At last I could talk to my siblings about junior high. But of course, my sister had just made it to ninth grade - and we had a four year high school system - so the conversation at the dinner table now revolved around high school. I was excluded once again.

I can remember going back to visit my favorite fifth grade elementary teacher, Mrs. Powers after going to junior high. When she asked me then if I had any plans to run for student government I was quite surprised. Huh? What do you mean? ME…be a leader?

Nooo - she must be joking, I thought. That wasn't allowed in my family, or at least that was the silent message I was receiving. It would make my siblings even more jealous toward me . . . and I couldn't have dealt with that.

In junior high my friends started to have boyfriends and they used the term "going together," whatever that meant. My mind never really went there and my friends never said anything else about it. Because of the deep sense of shame that was inferred in my upbringing, especially toward anything sex related, I never cared. I didn't want to think about it. I did wonder why I didn't have a special "boy" friend once in a while, but I soon began to reason that it must be because I wasn't very cute. Since no one in my life was telling me otherwise, I assumed this reasoning to be true.

There was one boy in seventh grade who did ask me to "go with him." I was still very naïve about all these matters. Since I knew so little about this whole realm, it seemed kind of scary to me and I told him no. That didn't sit very well with him. The next trimester we were placed right next to each other in science on the seating chart - right in the front row (oh no...I groaned inwardly). He teased me mercilessly. It was my payback I suppose.

Seventh grade indeed turned out to be a bad year. Not only did I have the experience with this boy, but I was also seriously injured for the second time in my life. The first time I'd fractured my ankle from a bike fall when I was in second grade. This injury was a little bit more traumatic. I was attacked by a dog - not just any dog - a St. Bernard. Man, was he HUGE. We were outside playing hide-and-seek one day after school and I made the mistake of getting within the distance of this big fella's leash. I knew when I heard his chain leash start to rattle across the ground, that I was in trouble and ran. I must have been only one or two more steps away from being outside his range, when he caught me by the leg with his jaw and whipped me around with such force that when I finally got free my clothes were torn and ruined. I was a mess. There was blood coming from my leg and face and grass stains everywhere from being rolled around as this humongous dog shook my leg back and forth with his jaw gripped around my lower leg. It was all I could do to hobble back to where my friends could see me. They went and told my mother and when she showed up, she yelled at me because I couldn't walk and had to be carried. To the doctor we went and about seven or eight stitches later on the front and back of my calf, I was on my way. But the wound was very deep and the swelling was so bad that I had to have crutches. That meant that I had to use the elevator at school. The kids all laughed at me and didn't believe me when I told them I was bit by a dog. I'm thinking "Why would I make this up?" It made no sense to me that these kids thought I was lying.

Somewhere around this time (in seventh or eighth grade), I met a new friend who gradually became another of my closest friends. To this day, I'm not sure why, because she was not a positive influence. Unfortunately, Paula liked to tell herself she was ugly and she spoke this out loud to those around her. I began to learn this from her and make the same verbal statements about myself that she did. What was really ironic to me was that though she claimed she was ugly, Paula had been through several boyfriends before I'd even had one!

I can remember wheeling this girlfriend Paula around in eighth grade in the teacher's chair in home economics class, one day. It was dark and we were in an adjacent classroom that was empty. I remember telling Paula there in the dark, "My parents are getting divorced." It was the first time I'd told anyone my big, dark secret and somehow it seemed symbolic to be telling one of my best friends in this dark room. It reflected my life and what my life felt like. Darkness - total darkness. I don't even remember her response or what else was said. But at least someone had listened and I was able to share my pain, for once.

That summer my grandparents were celebrating their fiftieth wedding anniversary in Iowa. My mother packed the four of us up and we drove from New England 1,200 miles to the Midwest. We visited with cousins and other family and got to see what life on Iowa farms was all about. We had a pretty nice time. I can remember saying to my mother in the car on the way home,

"That was fun. When can we go back?" She responded with a laugh and said, "It might be sooner than you think." That was the foreshadowing of the most devastating event in my life yet to happen - we were soon going to move.

It would take years to adjust and recover from the shock of it. This was worse than walking into my dad's apartment after my parents separated and finding another woman sitting on the couch in his living room. Apparently, everyone else in the family knew he was having an affair, but nobody bothered to tell me or seemed to think it was important to fill me in on this tiny little detail. They just let me walk right into it - into his new life and this reality of information, with no warning.

Now, I had to leave my home, my friends, my school, my father and everything else familiar to me. The weight of what I took with me, could in no way match the weight of what I'd lost. I was devastated by the move and humiliated about not knowing of my father's extracurricular activities as well. I'd never considered the idea that my Dad might be an alcoholic. Suddenly that thought seemed unavoidable in light of his new life. So, my dad was a drunk, my parents split up because he was having an affair and then to top it off, we were moving to Iowa! Wasn't life grand! I was still in a state of shock from the divorce, when we moved.

Well part of me, my mind, my thoughts and my emotions just refused to move along to Iowa with the rest of my body. That was my hometown, and it always would be. Those were my best friends, my school, that's where my dog was buried in the backyard. That was my house, my neighborhood, my life as I knew it. The memories lived on inside me, even though the life had ended. I would never forget who I was, at that time, and so I held on to the only thing I had - the memories.

My mother decided to have a garage sale for the things that weren't going to move with us. "Can you just sell me too Mom?" I thought. I don't wanna go. "How can you tear me away from the only home I've ever remembered after you promised me we wouldn't have to move? How could this be happening to me?" I was so scared. Sandy wrote in my year book at the end of the year that she still had a few ideas on how she could keep me there, in Northbridge. She even offered to let me stay and live with her for the school year. I know her parents would have let me. They were so welcoming and generous. Their house was the revolving door on the block that every kid went in and out of (and quite often got ice cream or some kind of treat during the visit). But of course, my mother wouldn't have any of that.

On our last night in Northbridge everyone in my family stayed at a friend's house. My Mom was at a neighbor's, I was at Sandy's and my brother and sister were elsewhere. Where, I'm not even sure. We loaded up the car. One of my other best friends, Kathy, rode her bike to Sandy's house to say goodbye. That meant so much to me. There weren't many words that I could choke out to anyone. The tears just wouldn't stop. I was just numb with disbelief. It was all I could do to climb in the front seat next to my mother and wave goodbye, as everyone gathered on the lawn. We drove by our beloved home once more - the sign in front that used to say "The Hallimans" and the house number "26," no longer swung from the pole in the front yard. Good-bye to life as I knew it. Good-bye to my home, my town, my friends, my school and all the security and comfort that had gone with it.

Life In The Country

Adjusting to Iowa was far more difficult than I could have ever possibly imagined. Hello to Iowa. I-O-W-A. It was easy to spell, but quite hard to remember apparently. For anyone having ever lived in New England, you know that life does not really exist beyond the Hudson River. I can remember the kids at school (in Massachusetts) asking me "Where is it you're moving to again? Ohio? Idaho?" They could never seem to get it straight. Yes, hello to Iowa. There was not much of a welcoming committee for us, at least that's the way it seemed to me. In fact, even the moving van was three weeks late. The only memory I have of that first summer there was my sister and I sitting on the kitchen counter (since we didn't have any furniture yet) watching Johnny Carson on the *Tonight Show* each night, on the tiny black and white TV we had brought along with us. I don't think we even had our own plates and silverware until the moving truck got there. And it was so blessed hot and muggy. I do remember that. Oh and the crickets. The crickets in my grandparent's house were plentiful for some reason. I remember one night waking up, turning the light on in my room, and there was a whole congregation of them that had invaded the middle of my bedroom floor. I screamed! I couldn't take it anymore, out there, in the middle of nowhere, with crickets and locusts buzzing all night and the hot summer air. I hated it.

Then school started. Little did I know that life was going to go from bad to worse, all on account of where I lived. What I realized later as an adult was, that it was all about money. My mother had promised us that we would not have to move. She made that promise particularly for me, because I was the only one left in high school. Well, when my father didn't pay his child support, we couldn't afford things. My grandparents offered us their house to live in and I'm sure it seemed like the only reasonable solution.

Which brings me back to where I lived; my mother was raised on a farm, but I certainly wasn't! Not only had I been transplanted from being hours within a REAL live beach and the ocean, to dry land, but I was stuck out in the country, with no civilization around me. I was miles from the nearest town and much more from the city where I was supposed to attend high school. In fact, the city was probably a good seven to ten miles away, which I wouldn't have minded except for the bus ride - over those lovely gravel roads. That was the next thing I had to contend with. Gravel roads. They didn't have those back East, at least not where I had lived. Gravel roads had never existed in my vocabulary until moving to Iowa. Everything was PAVED. To some people, this may not seem like a big deal. But it was to me. And for someone who had already learned, unfortunately, to cut herself down in appearance, dirty, grimy gravel dust didn't help the femininity in me blossom. My hair always felt coated with dust, which then left me with the alternative of washing it every day.

This might not have been such a bad alternative. But as luck would have it, my grandparent's house used well water. Rusty well water, in fact, which didn't leave me feeling too clean. It even coated the shower stall in a pale terra cotta colored stain, it was so prevalent. I don't know how people in biblical times managed without running water, quite frankly. I like modern day luxuries.

So! It was off to school every morning about 7:00 a.m. and then home sometime around 4. Back East I was off the bus after fifteen minutes and in the door a minute later, so this was a small nightmare to me. First the gravel roads and then the rusty water and now I had to wait an hour before I could even get home from school? Because of the rural setting we lived in, the junior high and high school were both bussed together. In order for our bus to make it to both schools, we ended up getting to school a half hour early, so the bus could still get the junior high kids to school on time. Then when we got on the bus after school, we had to go pick up the junior high kids before we even got to head for home. Wow. Life sure had changed.

I still have the memory of that first day I stepped on to the bus. The bus just pulled right into the semi-circle driveway and stopped at the door. It was almost surreal to me, to have my school bus pulling up to the doorway, way out in the middle of nowhere, with a corn field for a view from the picture window in our living room. The only positive thing I can say is that I had the luxury of waiting inside on cold winter days, instead of traveling down a long farm lane to reach the end and wait in the cold, unforgiving Iowa wind chills.

I had gone to registration at my new high school by myself. Actually if I recall correctly, my grandmother gave me a ride and waited outside in the car while I went through the process alone (I probably wouldn't have wanted her to go inside with me in reality, but I already felt so abandoned and going through everything alone didn't help). So, I knew a little bit about where I was going. But I stepped up on to the bus that first morning and sat down in one of the first seats I saw. The bus was pretty empty. And there was dead silence. They all looked at me and stared. No one said a word. You probably would have been able to hear a pin drop, save for the rumbling of that old bus as the driver grinded the gears and we pulled out of the driveway. Today, if faced with the same situation, I would smile at the kids and maybe crack a joke. But I was fifteen and my self-esteem felt like nothing. I rode in silence, turned my eyes east and remembered the world I had left.

Upon getting to school that very first day, I found my locker and somehow killed time until "first hour." That was another thing! Why couldn't the school be normal and just call it "first period?" Well, at the appointed time of 8:00 a.m., there I was looking hopelessly at the door of my assigned classroom and it was pitch dark. Nobody was in there. I didn't know what was going on. Someone walked by and said "Let's go, time for assembly." Huh! (too bad they'd forgotten to tell me at registration I was supposed to be in the gym). Hmmmm. I didn't know where I was going, but I just followed the guy and eventually ended up where all the students were! I don't recall a word that was said or who spoke at that assembly. I was just numb.

I knew sooner or later things would have to get better. I began to make a few friends, from the limited selection available. There was a set of identical twins that made me laugh and it was a welcome relief to have things to laugh about. Life was not that joyous at home. My sister had gone off to college in the fall and my brother was not home much since he was at college in Iowa City. It was a very lonely and empty time for me. After our parents' divorce, my sister is the one who spent any time with me and now that she was gone, I didn't even have that. Of course, when it was the four of us together as a family unit, she was always more drawn to my brother, since they were just a year apart in age.

As we had grown older, my sister had begun to tolerate me more and spend time with me. In the last year or two before moving to Iowa, we had grown closer. Once she got her license she would drive me places and with Sherry at the wheel, that was quite often an adventure in itself. My sister invented her own winter sport with the car called "snowbanking." She would drive into a snowbank at any opportune moment, with no warning. Did we ever get stuck? Not when I was with her, but it always made the ride more entertaining!

Then there was the infamous trip to Hampton Beach, New Hampshire when my mother was driving. My sister, her friend Holly, my mom and I were in the car. We had pulled up to a window to pay our toll. It was just a drop-in toll with no attendant, one where you throw the quarter in the bucket and go. It should be very simple, right? Well, my mom missed the bucket and had to get out of the car to pick up her coin. It was quite hilarious as we all ducked to make it look like she was traveling alone. On that same trip it started to rain on the way home, and our windshield wipers were broken. We had to drive down the turnpike in the rain, without any wipers, when Holly turned and saw another car without their wipers going and said, "Look they're doing it too!!"

That was quite a day. We laughed even harder about the wipers than the toll booth.

From spending more time with my sister, her friends had gotten to know me too and I really felt included by them - they LIKED having me around, much to my own surprise. I got pretty close to one friend of hers in particular, Joyce. My sister and Joyce decided to "get me out of school" one day to play hooky with them. Well, back East the schools didn't have open campus, so they wrote a note and went into the office and told them they were taking me to a "doctor appointment." But when the office buzzed my classroom and the teacher told me someone was here to take me to my appointment, I (like a dummy) didn't realize the scheme and said "I don't have an appointment!"

I was so naïve and honest, I didn't even get to skip school! We laughed and laughed about that later . . . and they both put in their yearbook memories at graduation . . . "Let's get Mia out!"

Sherry had been the greatest source of comfort to me, in our family and it was quite an adjustment having her away at college. The house was much quieter and if it weren't for her, our broken family would not have found as many ways to laugh. Laughter is a wonderful gift from God - it makes the heavy things lighter and helps you let go and heal.

My mother had bought a cocker spaniel puppy as something to ease the pain I was in, or so I guessed, and I had named her Buffy. Buffy was my solace during this time, I could love her unconditionally and she loved me back all the time, no matter what I did.

We had left Massachusetts in June and by April of the next year, my mother was hospitalized once again for severe depression. I was already so shut down from the sadness of moving and the loss - this just added to it. As usual, I spent much of my time alone, or on the phone with friends. My brother drove me up to the hospital once to visit mother, but I can recall leaving there and thinking I didn't want to ever visit again. It was devastating. My mother didn't say a word. She just stared at the floor. Here I'd devoted my childhood and my time at home to keeping the peace and trying to atone for her unhappiness (as if I was the cause of it), by cooking, cleaning and doing anything I could to help her out - and she was depressed anyway. I really did feel as if I were responsible for her happiness in a sense, because I was named after her dad and I was just like her. It was almost as if her being unhappy was a reflection of me and whether I was a good child or not. At least that's the way it felt at the time.

Participating in sports back East was something I had always done, but now here in Iowa that too was different. It was so frustrating. They didn't play field hockey. The fall sport in Iowa was volleyball, which didn't interest me much because we'd never played it competitively back East. Then there was basketball. Yes, I had always been a shooting guard and really wanted to play. But once again, there was that good old Midwestern catch: they didn't play five on five like every other school I'd ever known. I couldn't believe it. Seems the girls program was still in the dark ages of playing half-court basketball with three on three. I understood how you were supposed to play, but I hated it.

Basketball to my knowledge had always consisted of running up and down the court and now, I could only dribble twice and not go past the half court line? This was too weird. As if I wasn't depressed enough, now a simple game that I was good at had different rules that were just weird. I never even finished the first season. I sprained my ankle and that was it for me for the season.

No field hockey, no basketball - that left softball! There was hope! I had always been pretty good - played just about every position with success except first base and catcher. But wait - softball for some reason was played in the summer. I realized later in life that because of living in a farm community, they didn't play in the spring like we did back East, because of planting season. It was the same with the start of school in Iowa. They started in August and got out earlier in the spring because of planting season. Back East we always started school the first Wednesday after Labor Day. I felt like I was going to school in the summer, which in reality, I was. I hated that too. Softball in the Iowa summertime heat was not my idea of pleasant either. I could not stand the heat and muggy humidity already, much less the thought of putting on a uniform and playing softball in it. What happened to the cool spring evenings of April and May back East? I was living in a Midwestern pit of hell, or so it seemed at the time. Swimming was the only bright possibility left, but as it turned out, the pool was across town and I didn't have any travel arrangements to get there. I didn't even mention it to my mother or try to work out a way to get rides, because history had seemed to prove that it wasn't going to happen. And I didn't want to burden her.

The only redeeming thing I found in Iowa was that I could drive sooner. In Massachusetts you had to be eighteen, but here, you could get a permit when you were fourteen and drive at sixteen. This was once again, due to the farming community. Kids needed to be able to drive at a younger age in order to help out on the farms. Didn't anybody understand I was a city kid? I did!! I felt like the world around me was enclosed in a glass bowl, and I was staring at everything from the outside - as if I was disconnected from it and not really present in the situation. It just didn't seem possible that this was what my life had become.

During my junior year I did start to drive to school after I turned sixteen. That helped to ease the "old gravel road" transportation dilemma. My mother knew I was unhappy, although I don't think she realized the extent of it. My friends knew I was miserable too. Years later, when I was reunited with my girlfriend Corinne from high school, she asked me, "Mia, you were so unhappy when you moved here - WHY are you still in Iowa?" I laughed, and said "That's the golden question!" I had moved out of state once after graduating college, to New Mexico to live near my sister, but moving was never going to change the way I felt inside, until I was healed. The depression I felt at moving was real, but I was also in denial of its effect on me, so I didn't know that was what I needed.

As my friends and I began to drive in high school, gradually I began to experiment with the usual things - drinking, smoking and drugs, because I was so unhappy and that's what my friends were doing! My motto became "This life really stinks so if nothing else, I'm gonna have fun." And I did! I started partying and meeting lots of new people and life was grand.

But on the inside I was crushed and broken. There just wasn't anyone present in my life to guide me to God, even though I needed to build faith. There were no role models or peers that took a deeper personal interest in me or my well-being.

Most of my girlfriends seemed to be dating people and while I had crushes, I really didn't date anyone until I was seventeen. I just had fun hanging out with my friends in groups. Sunday nights were a blast. We'd go to a dance club in Iowa City where it was teen night and have the whole floor to ourselves. Line dances were popular and we always had so much fun.

Even though it was a bar, on Sunday nights they didn't sell any alcohol and turned the place over to the teenagers. My friends and I had met a group of guys from our "cross-town rival" City High and so it seemed like we spent a lot of time going back and forth between the two schools.

School itself was okay. The more I lived in Iowa though, the more I just wanted to get out. I wasn't comfortable. My sophomore English class was so uncomfortable for me that I transferred out, upon finding out that I was going to have to get up and speak in front of this group of peers - none of whom spoke to me. I wasn't going to do it. What I didn't realize then but I know now is that that was a direct result of the way my family unit had communicated and excluded me. I could not say a word to the group I'd been put with, because I'd been conditioned to being ignored, and thinking no one wanted to listen. They didn't speak to me and I didn't speak up - it was the same old dynamic from my family. It was the norm for me, it was all I knew, so I had accepted it.

The twist in this class was that now I was supposed to speak. How in the heck could I feel like I had anything of value to say to these Iowa kids - if my own family who was supposed to love and nurture me didn't seem to care what I had to say? I had such inner turmoil. I didn't dislike any of them, I just felt like they didn't like me. It was such irony. My English teacher knew how unhappy I was and she agreed to meet with the principal and let me leave the class for the second part of the course.

Transferring out of that English class, began a series of avoidance behaviors in my life that I wasn't aware I was starting. Little did I know the chain of events that would be set in motion, which would lead me from one disappointing heartbreak to another. And there was more of that to come, than I could have ever imagined.

Young Love

November 3, 1978

It was an early November day when I had reached the sweet young age of sixteen, that I got my first kiss. It was such a memorable moment and I was so happy to receive positive attention from a boy that I went home and started a journal; a journal of all the things in my heart and mind that I wanted to express over that moment. I knew this wasn't love or some big romance, but it was a boost to my self-esteem to realize I was attractive to someone. The kiss was from a fellow whose nickname was 'Duke.' I decided that I kinda liked that - it made me feel a bit like royalty, which given the circumstances at home (feeling invisible), I needed. 'Duke' and I never went out on a date after that and I never pondered why. I guess he knew that I wasn't too attracted to him. He must have just had the desire to kiss me and that was it. So he did. He kissed me right there in the hallway at school while we were wasting time during a free hour. My girlfriend Corinne giggled at me and pulled me aside afterward and whispered "Was that your first kiss?" I smiled and laughed. My innocence must have been obvious. It's true I didn't spend much time thinking about boys or romanticizing about dates and kissing and all that stuff because my mother had scared me off of those thoughts through one masterful manipulative method: avoiding the topic. She never talked about any of that stuff to me. Granted, I realize she probably was raising me exactly the way she'd been raised, but that didn't increase my knowledge or understanding of the mysteries of being a woman or help in my development. All of it scared me. So I didn't think about it. That seemed to be the coping mechanism (at the time) that worked best for me - denial. I certainly had the Cleopatra Syndrome down well - Queen of Denial.

A few months later I found myself at a party all bummed out over some guy who wasn't going to be there. I remember ending up sitting in the bathroom while this fellow Bob told me how cute I was and that I shouldn't feel bad. Little wonder that within a week or so, I went on my first date with him.

One of my best friend's was dating a friend of Bob's so it was one of those situations where it all seemed to make sense. It seemed like all of my friends were sleeping with whomever they were dating and that it was no big deal to them. Even though I wasn't raised in the church and had no theological understanding of why, deep down I knew this was something I did not want to happen. I wanted to save myself for marriage and be pure. Many years later I would come to understand the reason why, but because I was a naïve teenager that was lost and wandering in the wilderness of life with no spiritual protection, I overlooked that feeling, even though I knew it was there. I didn't give place to it and I didn't heed what my heart really longed for. I gave into the peer pressure instead. What did I know about love? Had I experienced genuine love and acceptance from my family? No. Did I have a father who had nurtured me along as a little girl? No. What did I know about love at age seventeen?

> *I must have thought I knew a lot because I gave away one of your most precious gifts Lord, to a young man who didn't deserve it and never honored it. I gave away the gift of my innocence. My purity, my wholeness, my oneness, my soul, my flesh, my spirit - all these things I gave away with the casual tossing into the wind. I gave that gift of innocence away Lord, as if it were a penny being tossed into a fountain, on a wing and a prayer. As if it wasn't precious enough to hang*

*onto or fight for. As if my own body and soul had no
value. Isn't that really the way I felt - as if I had no
value? Dear Lord, I was so young, I did not recognize
that as my creator, You love me exactly the way you've
made me, with your own Divine love.*

Looking back now I realize I was searching to add some sort
of feeling of value or worth to my life and having a boyfriend
seemed to be the way to do it. Alone I didn't feel very valuable.
My family didn't seem to think that my unhappiness was of great
concern, I guess. Since no one offered much support I figured
there was nothing I could do. After my parents divorced my
father had moved away and rarely even kept in contact with us.
My brother never talked to me much, or showed any interest in
being the big brother I so desperately hoped for. My sister was off
to college now. My mother was there in that she provided for me,
my earthly needs, but I was alone most of the time at home and
no one seemed to notice. So my friends and now Bob filled my
time and attention.

There were other activities I had been involved in that would
have helped avoid this pitfall of fleshly pleasure, but since we had
moved to Iowa from Massachusetts, nothing had been quite the
same for me.

I had always been a talented athlete and an "A" student, but
things in Iowa were different. There were no more sports to play
that fit with who I'd always been. There were no more summers at
the club, not even a "neighborhood" to play in, because we were
out in the boonies. It was not a bright and cheery world I moved
into. I had Olympic dreams and I knew I had talent. Everything
I tried came easy to me - I just needed a mentor to get there. I
had an expectation that my family would fulfill this need, but
nobody encouraged me. I didn't realize that it was "up to me" to
make things happen. Little wonder that I fell down a path that
was heading to despair.

I couldn't literally feel the pain Lord, but it was there. In my chemistry, in my soul, in my being, it was there. I had suffered as a child quite a bit more than I even knew, or understood, and the groundwork had been set for things to roll up into a total nightmare.

Unprepared

July 9, 1980

It was the summer after my high school graduation and I was busy being unprepared for the great big life changing event on my horizon: college. I could have cared less. Making my way in the world was of no concern to me, since life barely existed in my mind, beyond age eighteen. I was more worried about whether the top I wore matched the colored stitching on my jeans, hanging out with my friends and partying. Yes, I was more into friends and socializing than my studies. Could anyone blame me? There I was at age fifteen, uprooted from my wonderful home and country club lifestyle that I'd known most of my life to be transported and unceremoniously dumped in the middle of farm country.

The social scene at school was not the most fun, especially the first year I was there. The kids seemed to have all known each other their entire lives. They didn't seem all that friendly. No one went out of their way to befriend me. Looking back, I realize they were waiting for me to break the ice, but I just wasn't capable. I was scared, lonely, depressed and devastated at how my life had changed. I felt so out of place. My clothes were from the East Coast and I seriously doubted if any of them had ever seen topsiders. During my junior year, when a girl transferred in from Florida, I got to know her right away - and it was so simple. She welcomed my friendship because we shared the same struggle. I wanted to extend to her, what I had hoped these Iowa kids would give to me - some kindness or support. So I stayed out of the mainstream and away from the limelight, even though the leadership and power within me was blindingly bright to those who recognized it.

Having a boyfriend filled a void and it did make me feel more valued. And while I probably talked myself into thinking I was happier and having a great time, partying and having fun with all my friends, deep down there was still a great deal of pain I was masking.

I had a teacher my sophomore year of high school who tried to pull me out of this pit of negativity I was in. He saw how I was feeling because of a paper I had written on Gertrude Stein. Mr. Anthony was his name and he was Greek. He was the first person to introduce me to baklava and the Greek culture. Before moving to Iowa, I had seen a movie about Jackie O's life called *The Greek Tycoon*, and since seeing that I had wanted to go to Greece. The scenery was gorgeous and the culture fascinated me. Mr. Anthony thought I had quite a bit of potential, it seemed, but I was too young and angry at life to recognize that his interest was sincere and he merely wanted to encourage me. I was mad at the world and couldn't see that. I rebuked his interest and yawned at the compliments he gave me about my writing, because I didn't believe my own talent in that area. Writing was nothing. It flowed out of me like pure water. I didn't see it as having any potential or value because of how effortless it was for me. I look back now and realize I didn't appreciate the *one* person who came along in my life and tried to encourage me, because I didn't value the gift that had been given to me.

I was definitely one of those teenagers who thought they knew all they needed to know and I wasn't open to his input. Finally it was time to go to Bradford in Dubuque for my college orientation. This was the last session they were offering so I figured I better go. I had already postponed the trip once because of my work schedule. It was early July, and stiflingly humid as Iowa summers always seemed to be. I checked into my dorm room and it was late - no sign of my roommate.

July 10, 1980

In the morning my roommate and I went to breakfast and our first session of the day. It was there in the conference room basement of McCormick Center that I first heard his name - Sam Stephens. I didn't think anything of it until later when Leslie, my roommate invited me to go drinking with a group of people. We ended up in Sam's parents' car. I remember it so clearly, almost as if it were yesterday. It was a brown Cadillac Seville. I made a comment about how Sam's parents must have bucks, while his sister Christy played with the visor and showed me how the lights worked on it. "Christy, quit showing off!" Sam yelled at her and she giggled. So we cruised around Dubuque in this luxurious Cadillac and drank some beers. It was interesting talking to new people. Sam was a journalism major from Chicago, Leslie was a music major from southern Illinois and the other fellow in our group was an art major named Christopher. He was from Peoria, which I found funny because my sister was going to college there at the time. We talked and drank. The more I talked to Sam, the more I realized that I had never met anyone like him before. I felt so comfortable with him. I didn't realize it at the time what an amazingly precious gift that was.

July 11, 1980

I went back home for the remaining few weeks of summer feeling exhilarated from having met Sam, and uneasy about my boyfriend at home. I knew long before meeting Sam that Bob and I were going to end and I think he did too, but he wasn't willing to accept that without a fight. At the end of July I tried to break up with him but he was so persistent in pursuing me that I gave in and saw him again for the few remaining weeks before I left for college. What a life-changing decision that would prove to be.

August 27, 1980

Freshman year at college started and the four of us that had met at orientation all went out the night before classes started. Sam and I ended up talking most of the night and when he offered to walk me home to my dorm, we made plans for our first date the next night.

Sam couldn't come up to my room to get me, because the dorm floors were locked, so I waited outside. I remember sitting outside the dorm on the cement ledge, swinging my legs over the end, waiting for him to pick me up. As he walked up the steps he said, "Mia?" and I said "Yeah." And he said "Oh, this is the first time I've seen you with your hair down. I didn't recognize you at first." I remember thinking how odd that comment was, because I felt like I'd known him forever, when actually, it had only been just a few days. We walked down the street to a nearby bar and drank some pitchers. I couldn't help thinking how cute Sam was, but it was mostly his personality that made him that way. We laughed at all the same things and I was quite content that he had chosen me over Leslie. Sam stood about five feet nine inches tall, with sandy brown hair, brown eyes and as he put it "a big schnoz." I never thought his nose was that big, but Sam always joked about it. He was just plain cute to me in so many ways, but most of all, he made me laugh.

Meeting Sam was like meeting your best friend and finding a relationship that you knew was going to happen. I took it for granted almost, because of that pure energy between us that was undeniably there and seemed to be timeless. Once I met him, it seemed like he had always been in my life. During that first week in college, the 'honeymoon' phase of our romance, Sam made a joke about Christopher wanting to go out with me too. I said, "I know. What should I tell him?" And Sam said, "Tell him you're seeing me." We both just smiled at each other. I wasn't accustomed to having more than one person interested in me at a time. I had grown a bit in confidence that yes, I actually WAS attractive, but Sam's interest in me pretty much sent me over the moon. It wasn't that he was drop-dead gorgeous..... it was everything intangible that we seemed to share together and I was giddy and exhilarated by his attention. I can't recall the exact moment when but somewhere along the line, I fell in love with him. I loved him like no one else since.

Heaven And Hell

One week later I found out I was pregnant. Bob knew he had betrayed me. Even though he knew I was supposed to go to college, Bob wanted to get married - and this was his way of trying to make that happen. He didn't mention marriage often, but he had given me a diamond ring the Christmas of my senior year, which I had accepted. I didn't go around pronouncing us 'engaged' because I knew I was still going to college, and there was no wedding planned. I knew that an engagement for four years of college was unlikely.

Bob had calculatedly asked me if he could buy me a ring for Christmas and I simply said yes. At the time, I didn't give that question much thought, I just figured he meant some sort of gemstone because that's what most young girls in high school had - if they had a ring at all, it was usually a star sapphire. Imagine my surprise when he popped open the box after getting down on one knee - and it was a diamond! Gulp. I'd already said that he could buy me a ring, I just didn't realize he meant get engaged along with it! I accepted it because I was an idiot, er, I mean, I didn't know what else to do. I loved him, but I also knew I was supposed to go to college the next year and I didn't see those plans changing. It was odd. We didn't discuss the implications of an engagement, I just accepted the ring because I felt that if I didn't there would be no more Bob in my life! I didn't want that either. He had cornered me on the whole deal and we just went on. The whole relationship had been based on manipulation - yet I was too nice to tell him to take a hike. Whenever I tried to break it off with him he would go off on some drug trip or threaten to kill himself. One time I actually found him home alone, in his room, with a gun. That scared me into hanging around. Bob knew how to manipulate me and he was good at it.

No wonder Bob had begged and pleaded with me in July when I had tried to break up with him. When I told him I was pregnant, he didn't even bat an eye. He didn't seem surprised, shocked, saddened or any other emotion for that matter. He off-handedly mentioned marriage, but not in the terms that a young pregnant girl needed to hear. He didn't say "I will love you forever and take care of you both." Oh no! There was no persuasion in his voice at all. Instead, what became imbedded in my memory was what he told me as I was laying there in the hospital - and that was "he didn't like the idea of murdering his child."

Well neither did I. But once again, I felt cornered into a decision I wasn't ready to make. Who was I kidding? I was too young to get married - too young to be pregnant - too young for any of the sin that had permeated into my life. My innocence was gone and now the innocent blood of an unborn baby would be shed over it.

Of all the options I had, there seemed to be only one obvious choice in my little eighteen year old mind: abortion. Could I go to my mother? She never talked to me about this stuff when I needed to hear it, so there was no way in my mind I could turn to her now. Did I dare have the baby out of wedlock and bring shame on the family? And quit college? If I dropped out of college then I wouldn't be fulfilling my mother's grand plan for me, and my sense of responsibility to please her overwrote the moral decision of choosing life for my baby. She always said her goal was to put us all through college. What about the human life inside me? Didn't this baby have a right to live? But how could I have this baby when I knew I couldn't trust the father and he had lied to me on numerous occasions? I knew in my heart the baby was conceived out of manipulation and lies, because Bob had said he didn't climax. And I, being young and inexperienced, ignored the indicators that he had. All these things came at me yet in a single instant I made the unalterable decision and chose abortion. And I have regretted that decision ever since.

When I called the doctor's office for the test results and the nurse told me it was positive, I hardly hesitated. There seemed to be only one option. I told the nurse I wanted to schedule an abortion and she was only too happy to oblige. There was no indication of what this traumatic event could possibly do to me, there was no one cautioning me to think about this decision more thoroughly and most importantly, there was no one standing in my way protecting the rights of the unborn child inside me. The Supreme Court had taken care of that when they legalized abortion in 1973. And that was part of my reasoning. If it was legal, then how could it be wrong? Doesn't our country create laws that are just and fair and morally right? In my simple mindedness I naiively thought that my beloved country was only going to pass laws that were good for its people. How wrong I was.

Back on the phone with the nurse, she scheduled my appointment as if it were a routine physical exam. Today my stomach churns at the thought of how lightly our society deals with abortion - at how acceptable and common it is. It is as if you can throw away something as miraculous as God's own creation - a baby - and feel no pain for it afterward. That is the biggest lie of abortion. It would take over twenty years to enlighten my thinking and realize this truth. For a few years, I was pro-choice and tried to comfort myself into believing their dogma - "it's my body and my choice." But that was just more denial. Deep down, I knew it was wrong to reverse the phenomenon of child birth.

September 12, 1980

I remember the feeling in the air of this morning clearly . . . It was a beautiful, crisp fall-like Friday morning and I was supposed to meet Bob down the street from my dorm at 7:00 a.m. Knowing how Bob handled things when they didn't go his way, I was quite concerned that he wouldn't show up at all. To my surprise his truck was sitting there in the empty lot as I walked up. I climbed into the truck and we drove to the hospital in a heavy silence. There were no words to speak.

A few hours later he dropped me off at the dorm. He tried to kiss me goodbye, but I was crushed and numb. I remember climbing out of the truck and walking away in utter shock and pain at what my body had just experienced - hoping it wasn't true, hoping it hadn't really happened, hoping that there was some way I could erase this horrible day from my life . . . I must have known subconsciously my baby was going to heaven, because even though I had no relationship with God then, I wore a yellow shirt. When I thought back on it later, in my mind the shirt represented the sun, and the heavens of God.

The next day I went to work and kept thinking, "I can't believe I'm here and life is as usual, even though there is one less child to be born in this world."

Little did I know that this decision would become a partial death sentence to my own soul. I would never be the same again. And for someone who had so little to build on as far as esteem and self-confidence, this was a crusher. Chemically, my body reacted very badly to the procedure and I was physically thrown into a state of chemical imbalance or panic attacks. Life went on about me - but nothing was ever the same again.

The abortion sent me into years of emotional and physical torment, anxiety, inner chaos and confusion that I simply could not manage. Anxiety and fear first began to grip me in class. College was supposed to be carefree and fun - and at times, it was. But I was also lost in my own private hell. The constant pounding of physical symptoms - my heart racing, my throat clenched, my chest swarming in fear, my ears ringing, my head pounding - all these symptoms were relentless, day after day after day. I couldn't get away from them. I tried everything I could to figure out how to breathe again, to try to refocus so I could think clearly and concentrate on school. Nothing worked.

My private hell became trying to understand what was wrong with me. How had everything turned to ashes overnight? Soon the anxiety spread from the classroom and isolated places to everywhere. Just a casual walk across campus became a nightmare for me. Eating in the cafeteria was another place where the level of suffering increased. It was difficult for me to breathe, so functioning at any capacity was always a challenge. I managed to get decent grades, despite the chaotic state I was in. However, decent grades were disappointing to me, when I knew I was an A student. I longed to just crawl inside myself and pretend I didn't exist and make the world go away. I couldn't stand the way I felt and I just wanted to die.

I had cried out to God during this time of pain, darkness and torment. I boldly demanded of a God I hardly knew: "What do you want from me?"

I couldn't stand the pain any longer and I didn't know what else to do. I had found a spiritual connection through my art history classes and all the Christian art we studied and had started praying regularly in college. But as the anxiety and torture wore on, I cried out to God, but heard no answer. I don't think I was even capable of listening in those moments. I mean, I couldn't quiet my body to hear anything. My mind was constantly swirling. I was consumed by the angst my body was in and I had no idea what to do.

So I just went on. Within my soul I frantically searched for solace and peace. I had no upbringing in the church. I believed in God, but I hadn't even heard or understood the message of salvation. I was doing all I could just to survive at that point in time. That was the only thing my life was about: survival. I didn't understand that Jesus was alive in heaven, watching over me the whole time, waiting for me to learn just how much He loves me.

Life And Death

Needless to say, September 12th signaled the end of my relationship with Bob. In the process of dating someone new and getting to know Sam, I had told him there was a chance I might be pregnant. I wanted to be honest with him, even though our relationship was not to that point. He was very understanding and appreciative of my honesty and also very supportive. He knew that this would be tough on me. He predicted it but he didn't discourage me either.

I knew almost instantly that I liked Sam in more than just a general "nice guy" kind of way. We clicked. We could finish each other's thoughts and sentences. Whenever I was alone with Sam, my fears and anxieties were greatly reduced and I felt safe. His spirit had a calming effect on me - it seemed like we were always in sync with each other's moods. I'd never had that with anyone before and to find it, seemed like such a gift from God. In fact, that's what I did to Sam. I put him right up there on a pedestal and worshipped him in my life more than anything else. It was a great comfort to have him to turn to. He loved me and supported me. His mere presence comforted me so, that I couldn't imagine life without him. I had always had this inner, unexplainable feeling, this prophetic "knowing," ever since my childhood, that there was one specific person God had planned for me. I thought for many, many years that Sam was that person.

On the academic side, I admired Sam too. He talked about how he got along with his instructors and joked with them like the class clown. I could never do that, and I admired him for his ability to speak up and be noticed. I was always the one cringing inwardly in the back. Despite my turmoil and anxiety, I still remained functional. "The family" as we called our group in college, liked getting high, (except me) and even though I wasn't always participating, I was still exposed to the smoke whenever they lit up and it always effected me. If I wasn't experiencing another panic attack or extreme discomfort then I was lethargic or burnt out from being around the dope smokers.

"The family" of friends who ate together, partied together and lived in the same dorm (except me) was made up of Derek, Kim, Christopher, Sam and I. Sam and Christopher were quite the pair. It turned out that they had the same birthday. It also turned out that Christopher had no roommate, which gave Sam the chance to move in with him. Good 'ol room 207. We called it "the mole hole," and anyone who hung out there was called a "mole" at one point or another.

Derek and Sam hit it off because they both loved playing guitar. Christopher was a very talented artist too. He was into drawing and printmaking. I loved his silliness. We had a beach party in the dorm basement one time and everyone was supposed to dress Hawaiian. Christopher made himself a surfboard and painted it with wild flowers, stripes and designs and carried it around all night. Sam and a couple other guys put on Hawaiian skirts and tube tops with plastic garlands around their necks. It was quite hilarious and a favorite memory of those days in the dorm.

Everyone in Sam's dorm was fun and at the time, I was happy to be able to move into his dorm our sophomore year. Then he wouldn't have to walk me home at night! We used to call Sam's resident assistant "Moses" because he really looked like Charlton Heston from the *Ten Commandments*. Their floor was pretty well known for their pot and Sam's room seemed to be a revolving door of "the family" and other people getting high.

By the end of our sophomore year it wasn't certain if Sam would be able to come back to Bradford next year or not. His parents didn't want to pay for him to go to college out of state anymore, since they lived in Illinois. They wanted him to stay at home and go to school from there; grades were a reason as well. One night as we were preparing to say goodbye for the summer, he said to me "You can consider yourself engaged if you want Mia." I knew what he meant. We had talked about living together before his staying in Chicago had come up, so I knew that Sam was saying he wanted to spend the rest of his life with me. He was reserving me for the future. The summer loomed ahead and it seemed like it was going to be pretty empty. The darkness and depression I felt facing this situation was heavy. I was still carrying depression from my childhood that I wasn't even aware of and adding this was a quite a weight. We kept in touch but not as much as I liked. He called me one night in early July and said "When do you want to get married?" I said I thought we'd get married the fall after we both graduated. And then he asked me where I wanted to live and how many kids I wanted to have. I knew this was just confirmation that he intended for us to be together. At the end of the conversation he even added "I have something for you," which I took to mean a ring, but I also knew he'd have to give it to me in person. I held that promise and that hope in me, and truly believed in faith that all our dreams would come true, one day.

Our junior year started and when I offered to move to Chicago so we could be closer to each other, Sam wouldn't hear of it. He also discouraged me from visiting and he hadn't been to visit me since the summer. Finally I couldn't take it anymore. I wrote to him and broke it off in October. There was never any closure in my heart, because I did not hear back from him. Thanksgiving, Christmas and New Year's passed and there was no communication between us. Valentine's Day passed - no word. Finally, it was March and with my birthday looming, I knew in my heart if I didn't hear from him then that it was indeed truly over.

March 11, 1983

Finally I received my answer - only it wasn't the one I had hoped for. Ten days before my twenty first birthday I received a phone call from his sister - Sam was dead. He'd gone into the garage, started his brand new blue Mustang convertible and let it run until the life was taken out of him. Whoa. I knew that his family wanted to believe it was an accident, but in my heart that didn't feel like the truth. Needless to say the tears didn't manage to shut off for days after that. My thoughts of him had never ended before and now they seemed to crush in on me more heavily. As if MY life hadn't already been dead enough, this was like putting another nail in my own coffin. The guilt I felt was unbelievable. At the unspoken apologies and sentiments of my heart that now I'd never have the chance to share. I had loved him more than life itself and he was gone.

As I lay in bed the night before, after being out drinking with friends, I kept hearing in my head, "Call Sam. Call Sam," It wasn't even my own voice, and I didn't know why I was hearing this all of a sudden. I'd determined in my own mind that I wouldn't try to contact him - that it would have to be him who contacted me if we were ever to communicate again. I was so stubborn and unforgiving. I knew that he'd been unfaithful to me and the trust between us had long been broken. I couldn't reconcile myself to marrying someone that I knew might be unfaithful again. But I believed he was my soul mate and that we were "meant to be together." I picked up the phone and punched in the number but hesitated. It was late - after midnight - and I knew his parents would probably hear the phone and wake up. And then they'd be mad at him. Finally in frustration I put the phone back in its cradle. As I lay back down, the urge to call him was still there, but I was tired and finally fell asleep. Now he was dead.

As if the anxiety I already had weren't enough, I now had this added emotional burden of guilt, sadness and pain. After our sophomore year when Sam left college, I had moved off campus to try to bring more peace back into my life. Even though the anxiety lessened, the move had really worked against me because it left me feeling more isolated and depressed. I still had friends, but I did miss being around people in the dorms and the cafeteria, even though these environments produced anxiety for me at different times as well. It was a catch-22 for sure!

As a freshman, I had bought a surrealist reproduction of *The Sacrament of the Last Supper*, by Dali, and put it on the ceiling above my bed. At night I would look up at this poster and pray, with no real understanding of the spiritual presence I felt. Somehow, I was comforted. As the anxiety and torture wore on, I cried out to a God I didn't really know or understand, for life to end . . . . I couldn't see any hope, I couldn't see any purpose . . . I was miserable, I screamed out loud to the silence from my tortured soul and asked . . . "What do You want from me?" All I wanted to do was die. But thank goodness my fear and lack of understanding prevented me from ever taking action on these feelings. When I was little, my mother would tuck me in and have me say a prayer:

> "Now I lay me down to sleep
> I pray the Lord my soul to keep.
> If I should die before I wake,
> I pray the Lord my soul to take, Amen."

It was this same prayer that made me think about death every night as a young girl. It worried me that I *would* die in my sleep. I had no theological understanding of what happened after you die. No one had explained the heaven part to me. I only knew I didn't like the 'if I should die' part of the prayer. This had created a fear of death in me and now Sam was gone. Throughout my young life I had often wondered who in my life would be the first person to die, and I just couldn't believe it. It was Sam.

When he was younger Sam was a very promising football player - a quarterback, no less. As a freshman in a private Catholic high school he already had college scouts watching him. But his dreams of playing collegiately or professionally would never become reality. Sam had a rare problem called sub-fluxation of the shoulder, which meant that his shoulder went out of joint. As in my own life, I'm sure the loss of being able to compete in sports was more devastating to him than anyone could have ever anticipated or imagined.

I got the phone call from Sam's sister on a Friday morning, the first day of spring break. I had plans to fly with a friend to Florida on Sunday and stay with my father for the week, but the funeral was set for Monday - what timing. I couldn't believe how this was all going to play out. His parents graciously invited me to stay with them for the funeral - his family knew how much we had meant to each other . . . his sister Lynn told me that Sam had talked about me all the time, but that I lived too far away. Because my girlfriend Cindy didn't seem too excited to fly down by herself to stay at my father's, and because I didn't think it was right to impose a stranger on Sam's family and their grief (and my own pattern of keeping everyone else happy), I made the decision to go on with our original plans. I think part of me was relieved to avoid the funeral anyway. I don't think if I attended Sam's funeral that I could have ever finished college. I don't think I would have been able to function for quite awhile after that. The funeral could well have been my own demise if I had gone and mourned with everyone else.

So Cindy and I went to Florida and I laid in the sun by the pool, not believing this was real, with tears rolling down my face every day. I couldn't believe that God had been so cruel to me. That he had taken away the person on this Earth who'd meant more to me than my own life. That he had taken away my hope of a meaningful future. I had been willing to give up everything for Sam – it was a rare love, a special bond and even though it wasn't perfect, I had never stopped loving him.

Flying home on my twenty-first birthday, we landed in Chicago and within hours I found myself looking at Sam's snow-covered grave, which was heaped two feet high with beautiful bouquets, now frozen and dead. He was so loved, so special, so funny, intelligent and yet so desperate to be free. He had said to me once "I want to fly Mia." Years later I thought back on that comment and realized he meant his spirit wanted to fly and be set free. It was then that I realized how alike we were – we had both felt trapped inside our earthly bodies.

Sam's grave was enough reality for me. It should have been a day for celebration, but instead it was indeed, the saddest day of my entire life. It was my golden birthday and I was clothed in a seemingly endless life of darkness and mourning. In some ways, it just didn't seem possible that my life could be filled with so much sadness. I had always thought or sensed subconsciously as a young girl that there was something important I was supposed to do with my life, yet at every corner, at every new season I seemed to be met with tragedy. This was my reality. This was my life. Years later I would look back and realize that as a child, I had seen this prophetic "darkness" in my life, by not being able to envision my life beyond age eighteen. I literally had no visions of what life might be like beyond that point in time. There were no childhood dreams of a future career, husband, family or home for me. Those things never occurred to me. I had always been inwardly bracing myself because of the darkness I was in, and the fact that I couldn't see out of it.

Once again, my family did little to support me during this traumatic time and back to college I went. I wanted to stop the world and get off, but life kept going. Part of me wanted to quit college and just take a break, but again my mother would not have supported me in that decision. I had already asked! It was all I could do to try to survive this too. There were days and times when I literally FELT Sam's presence with me, even his voice, calling me to be with him. I missed him so much and we were so close spiritually, that this was very real to me. Suicide was not an option that I seriously entertained in my mind for any length of time, but because of Sam, it hung over me like an ever-present shroud.

Somehow, my senior year in college arrived. I had enrolled as an interior design major in the College of Fine Arts. It was the architectural part of the program that I enjoyed and hoped to put into practice. I'd asked myself if this was the right major for me since I was not an accomplished artist and the program was in the College of Fine Arts, but I had chosen it and there I was trying to stick it out. Sam had been a journalism major and since he knew I wrote in my own personal journal he tried to encourage me to switch to journalism. My roommate at that time had a double major of art and advertising, which really was the ideal combination for me too. I knew I should have gotten a double major and eventually I did add journalism classes as a minor, but each time I looked over the required core classes for a journalism major, there was one class that made me cringe: Speech. In fact, I never changed my major to journalism because of it. My future didn't concern me, because I was too busy just trying to survive. The thought of having to go through the ordeal of giving a speech in the extremely paranoid and uncomfortable state I was usually in, was not something I felt up to tackling.

Each and every day was pure hell for me as it was and I had yet to find any relief or constant source of comfort from this daily torture. All I wanted to do was get out of college. It hadn't been the most pleasant of experiences for me. Even graduation itself was a bust. After spending thousands of dollars to brighten the yellow brick road of my future, I was rewarded with a tassel on my mortarboard that was brown. Not that I have anything against the color brown, but hey, everyone else had a vibrant blue or red or purple or yellow tassel. As a fine arts major, color (in this circumstance) really seemed to matter at the time, and I was not too pleased with my very expensive brown tassel. To top it off, who should I see at the end of the ceremony but my old roommate that had tried to break Sam and I up. We greeted each other but there was nothing to say. It was just a reminder that there was one person missing from that day. And I still felt his spirit with me.

It took years of depression, medication and self-help before I was ever able to let go of feeling personally responsible for Sam's death. The Lord finally showed me that it wasn't just my harsh words or our separation and break up that led to his actions; it was a culmination of many different things in his life, including the loss of fully using his arms. Jesus Christ through his magnificent power and grace has carried me through this and made me an overcomer. Without Him I know I would not be here to tell this story.

Real Life

I praise God that He has carried me through it all. I know it's only by His hand that I live. After miraculously graduating from college though, the walls seemed to close in on me further. My goal (actually it was my mother's) had been reached. I had gotten my degree. Now, I only left the house to go to work and the store - that was it. Even my brother, who I was sharing an apartment with, noticed and told me I needed to get out of my room. Well, it wasn't quite that easy.

Later on in life, I would discover through a prayer ministry the root cause of all my fear and what caused me to go into such severe anxiety after my abortion. There were several events really. The first was when I was three years old and I was hit just above the eye with a golf club. I'm not sure this was an accident and as a small child, this would set the course for me to "stay out of the way" and keep the peace.

Next was the memory of being thrown into a dark closet, with a heavy blanket over my head, at the age of eight or nine. Fear invaded the moment when I started to choke and cough and I realized I was actually being smothered. It was the first time I experienced real terror and panic. But I blocked it out because I couldn't bear the pain and reality of the fact that someone disliked me. Imbedded in my mind from that memory and my inability to process it was the reality that I couldn't breathe. It was a memory I completely blocked out for most of my life, but the Lord uncovered it and replaced it with His truth - that He was with me always and He is the very breath I breathe.

As a senior in college, I had tried to check myself into the hospital because of extreme depression, anxiety and discomfort. By this time, I just wanted some relief from this hellish existence, but even the hospital would not admit me. They said I displayed no signs of a mental breakdown. I had tried to get professional help once and got no support from my family. What about my mother? My mother loved me, I knew, but was she there for me? I needed her so desperately and she wasn't there for me. My sister had the 'middle child' syndrome and the fear of being overlooked, I suppose. But there was no overlooking Sherry. She was my hero in many ways. She sought attention and I let her have it because I loved her and I knew she needed it. In return she did take me under her wing and offered me more comfort and acceptance than anyone else. When my brother or anyone else was around - it was every kid for themselves - and I was doomed because I chose not to fight for the attention. I gave into what everyone else wanted and - just to keep them all happy.

So, everything always seemed to feel like it was my fault. Subconsciously, I began to feel sorry that I'd ever been born. I began to wish that I'd never been born and in order to keep everyone happy, I was the quiet little daughter/sister, who did what everyone wanted. I shut up, I kept quiet because I didn't want to make any waves, I was too afraid of the pain speaking up might cause me (ie - a golf club in the eye, or being smothered in a closet). There were times I'd cry myself to sleep in total sadness and not fully understand why. I couldn't face the fact that my family for the most part, seemed to always reject me. I buried the truth because it probably would have been more than I could handle at that young age. Looking back I see how these family dynamics are not uncommon. But to me, they were devastating. I needed someone to go to bat for me, to step in and say "Hey, we have got to get you some help," but that just didn't happen. My mother was so burdened herself, that she couldn't. I see all this more clearly now and I have found peace and forgiveness. But at the time it felt almost as if I'd wandered in the desert nearly as long as Moses.

Eventually I would leave Dubuque and return to Iowa City where I'd gone to high school. I found a job there and began meeting new people that were a lot of fun. I also embarked on a deeper and more spiritual life when a friend introduced me to a Bible fellowship church. It was difficult at best, having discovered God, while still in the throes of severe anxiety. It left me feeling unable to reach out and become firmly rooted in a church (while I was in Iowa City), though I did go to a weekly Bible study on Monday nights. Finally one day while I was praying I understood the Lord to say "Bloom where you are planted Mia." This gave me a lot of comfort. I wasn't into any extreme lifestyle but because of my increasing faith, I began to think something more of me was required than what I was doing. This word from God brought me comfort and I went forward with my life as I understood it should be lived. I had just moved into a townhouse that I was sharing with three other girls and had started dating someone new and in fact, things seemed to be on an upswing. But still, there was more tragedy on the way.

Finding Faith

February 3, 1987

It was an early Tuesday morning and I was getting ready for work in my crowded little (as yet unpacked) room at my new townhouse. The phone rang. It was my mother on the other end. In a broken voice she choked out the message that my uncle (her brother) had killed himself the night before. Once again, there was utter shock, disbelief and guilt. I had just seen my uncle unexpectedly the Saturday night before, but had not spoken to him. I had been out on a date with George and we had decided to just go driving around out in the country, in the area near my mother's house, for some goofy reason. George was pretty goofy so I never tried to make much sense out of some of his ideas. It didn't seem like we'd driven a long time but all of a sudden George realized we were going to run out of gas, if we didn't find some pretty quick. We were miles from the closest town and it was so late that nothing was open. I remembered that my uncle had a gas tank on his farm and told George that he'd probably give him a couple gallons if he went up and asked, so he did. In my embarrassment, I hid in the front seat, knowing my uncle well enough to know he'd never let me live this down. Sure enough, as I'd predicted my uncle was a good guy and like most farmers, he did what I knew he would and gave George some gas. It was the last time I would ever see him or hear his voice and now, he too, was gone. My uncle, like my grandfather, was charismatic in his own way as well. He had the gift of gab and so often did he use the word "Mercy" in place of "Oh my gosh," or "Wow" that he became known by this nickname. I do believe that he was offering up a prayer for his own soul each time he exclaimed it, having also been depressed for many years.

People asked me if I was "close" to my uncle. He wasn't like a father to me, but he was family. I loved his humor and his military haircut that he always wore, before it was ever in style. He left a wife, two children and a granddaughter. It didn't matter to me, how "close" we were, it was tragic any way you looked at it.

It had been less than four years since Sam's death and now to go through the same barrage of guilt and disbelief all over again was unexpected and depressing. I had been on medication at various times for depression, ever since first seeking counseling in Dubuque after my abortion. Nothing really seemed to have that much of a positive effect, but knowing my genetic inheritance from my mother and her history of depression, I believed that it was a necessity.

One of the friends I'd made had introduced me to a new bible study group in Cedar Rapids that I started going to regularly. I'll never forget the leader, Bea. She was so godly and grounded. She had so many different versions of the Bible that it boggled my mind. I never knew there were that many and she referred to all of them: The Amplified, the Revised Standard, Scofield's, plus a Bible encyclopedia and dictionary. She was the one who prophesied that she saw my hands writing. Bea was right. During my entire lifetime of pain, turmoil and anguish, I had kept my journal, which I had started on that autumn day when I was sixteen, after my first kiss. I had notebook after notebook filled with the entries of my days. I felt that I was supposed to write about Sam and the tragedy of that loss, but I could never get myself motivated to work on it seriously.

Because of Bea's prophesy, I enrolled in a correspondence course for *Christian Magazine* writers. Although I was more functional than I'd ever been since my abortion, I still couldn't stand the thought of going into a classroom again. Taking the course through the mail was "safe" and I could hopefully fulfill my purpose this way. As a result of this course, I began to do free-lance writing for a local publication and was even published in the magazine *Christian Single*.

My relationship with God was based on a lot of guilt and fear, but as I began to use scripture to fight my fear, things improved. I was using my religion and my faith to hide from and manage my fear and agoraphobia, but I still was not healed and released from the past. I still had more tragedy and grief ahead - more than I ever expected. Considering what I had already survived, I kind of figured that my lot in life was for things to improve and that the depression and darkness had reached its limit. Good times were ahead. I thought my quota of pain had been filled. Jesus was in my life and my heart and somehow I believed that the severity of my sorrow had to end at some point! Enough is enough, I thought! But still God's love had not permeated my mind. The depth of my anxiety was not healed and my relationship with God was not all that healthy. I was involved with the singles group at church, had plenty of friends and activities, but it was a constant battle to keep myself involved. I felt like I took my spiritual life much more seriously than everyone else around me and it seemed like there was no place where I really fit in. I wanted to commit my whole life to Him. In fact, it seemed like I would have to go back to bible school to continue down the path I was on, but I was bound by my fears and not fully convinced of the call God had on my life. Every time I stepped out to do something, the anxiety symptoms would flare up, making it extremely uncomfortable for me to even go and worship - yet that is where I longed to be: in the presence of God. I felt His peace in my spirit and I wanted more of it.

In my newfound spirituality, I was pretty upset by the standards that I saw other singles living by. Several instances of promiscuity around me would become a stumbling block, in my legalistic mind at the time. I did not see the godly example I expected of people around me, living according to His Word, and I left the church that had brought me closer to God than I ever knew possible, and I left in utter disillusionment. My conclusion was that if the Christians I saw around me weren't even living according to the Word, then it just didn't matter. I had not left my spiritual relationship with God, just the church, and in my own heart and mind, I always knew God was still with me.

November 14, 1989

A few months after leaving the church, I was introduced to the man I would eventually marry. Although Pat had been married before and had a daughter, that didn't deter me. In fact, his daughter swayed me more than I knew. She was my "replacement child," the daughter I had aborted nine years earlier. I loved her dearly and to this day, still do. She was the flower girl in our wedding . . . . . and ceremoniously dropped the petals down the aisle, after the ceremony! Our wedding day in October of 1990 was beautiful and I treasure the memories.

Faith played a big part in my decision, and I was ecstatic to learn that Pat had been raised in the church, and that his father was a retired minister. We had gone to church in the beginning of our marriage but when we moved to the opposite side of town, and things got difficult between us, our attendance began to dwindle and we didn't make it on a regular basis as I'd expected and hoped.

The biggest blessing that came out of the marriage was our son. God did bless us with a child and despite the financial stress of our situation, the time I had at home with him in his first six weeks of life are most precious to me. Born in early February, Andrew, as he was finally named, was my Valentine baby. At the time we had a crank swing that he loved to sit in and would often fall asleep. When I'd start the swing again, the noise would wake him up and he'd flail his arms when he heard the sound, then fall right back to sleep. He also loved bath time and I was so proud he never got an ear infection for the first two years of his life.

My marriage to Pat only lasted a few years, before we separated in March of 1994. I begged and pleaded with Pat to get counseling for some issues. My mother wrote him a letter, doing the same, for the sake of the children. But my pleadings were to no avail.

Being a single mother with a toddler and dealing with a divorce was not something I had anticipated or ever care to repeat. At the time, I was starting my first salaried position after being out of college ten years, and the reality of dealing with legal matters was very nerve-wracking and unpleasant for me. I thought that my marriage had been built on godly values. I had married him in faith and trust, despite some indicators that it might not be a good idea. I guess when your car breaks down on your way home from the rehearsal dinner, you might want to think things over a little more carefully! But I was too proud to call it off at that point, and now, here I was with another situation I was unprepared for. It was very disillusioning to wake up and realize that I had not married the right person. But then, I still thought the "right" person that God had planned for me was already dead, and had often wondered if I would be alone anyway. Pat played on the mercy in my heart and I fell for it. He talked about how he'd been taken advantage of and treated so poorly by his first wife and in my mind, I replaced everything he had lost: a home, a child and other material things. I thought I was quite the shining example of goodness and kindness and he just took advantage of it and used me as a tool of revenge to payback all the hurts from his first marriage. I'm not perfect either, but that is how it felt at the time. I was left in such a deep financial hole. I felt he still loved his first wife, and probably always would, even when I married him. But I was very much comforted by Pat's spirit and clung to that as a basis for love and happiness. It is hard to make sound decisions when life has thrown you so much turmoil, and since I'd never found true healing from my abortion, this would prove to be another choice, that I thought was right, which turned out to be wrong.

Once again, instead of turning and running toward God, I let other people and their actions turn me the other direction, away from the very one I needed. I felt like I'd gone full circle. My motto became once again "Well, this really stinks and once again life is not turning out as I expected, so I'm gonna have fun," only this time I was older The people around me were doing the usual things - going to happy hour after work, etc. I was just along socializing for the most part, since I'd never been a fantastic drinker. And then God would unexpectedly bring someone into my life that would shake me deeper than anyone ever had, since Sam.

July 10, 1996

We were headed to the baseball game on this particular night to hang out on the terrace amongst the beer drinkers. I remember it so clearly. My girlfriend and I had only been there a short time when he walked past me and said "Hi!" That never happened to me, and I don't know why. Guys just didn't walk up to me and casually start a conversation, or say hi as they were walking by either. I was in shock that he'd said anything to me at all. He was so handsome... with dark hair, dark eyes, a great voice and personality to match.

We were on our way to the restrooms and when we got back there he was - standing right across from our table. Pretty soon Jeremy was over at our table, sitting down and we ended up talking most of the night. The more I talked to him and the more I discovered we had in common, it became very easy for me to think that "Ta Da!" God had magically replaced all my losses . . . . the loss of my true love Sam, the lost relationship with both my father and brother. Jeremy was a golfer, just like them. He had played golf for the University of Iowa, just like my brother. He had lived in Chicago, just like Sam. His favorite golf course was Medinah, the one my father had worked at when I was first born. On and on the list of coincidences and common ground went.

But Jeremy was scared of having a relationship at all because of his own past. There were many coincidences that I saw as signs but Jeremy did not practice much of a spiritual life and he would never comment on the things I saw as pointing us toward belonging together. And again, there was a presence, a spiritual connection and power between us that seemed almost tangible at times and so reminiscent of Sam. Meeting Jeremy was like a re-awakening and a reminder of what Sam and I had once had. It seemed like a cruel irony to have that kind of powerful connection brought to me once again, to have it dangled in front of me like a carrot on a stick, only to be held at a distance and not be able to get to know him better. We had only dated a few times before it became obvious (as he himself admitted to me) that he was on the run from everyone and everything – especially the past.

God was knocking on my door again, when he brought Jeremy into my life. I had gone back to reading scriptures and renewing the Word that I had already placed in my mind some six, seven years earlier. Jesus had never turned away from me. He watched every step I took while I was away from a deepening relationship with Him, knowing full well what His plans were (Jeremiah 29:11). That someday He would bring me back. He walked beside me the whole way. He walked beside me and probably even carried me through the next tragedy that was about to hit my life, full force.

February 4, 1997

It was another Tuesday and I was going about the business of work when I got a phone call in the afternoon from my girlfriend Julie. Her and I were both single parents and we had been friends a couple of years. We socialized a lot together and liked going out dancing. Julie had stayed home with her son that day because he was sick. Just the day before at work she had talked to me about her boyfriend Mitch and some of the problems going on. Mitch was an ex-Marine, a green beret and he was also doing undercover work for the local police. She told me how depressed he was and that he had a gun (of course because of his job). Just yesterday in their conversation, Julie said he had mentioned killing himself. When I answered the phone she said to me "Mia, remember the conversation we had yesterday about Mitch?" I said "Yeah." She said "He's got the gun out and he's threatening to kill himself. Call 911." She hung up and I called 911. I called Julie back an hour later and Mitch answered. When I asked for Julie he said, "She's outside." So I just said "Ok, tell her I called," and hung up.

Little did I know that Julie had fled with her son and Mitch was barricaded inside in a stand-off with the police. Sometime after that, he decided to take the phone off the hook and I could never get through on the line again. Hours later, the police finally broke in and found him dead - the third person in my life to commit suicide.

This last event, along with everything else in my life that I was carrying, landed me in the hospital two months later, in a severely depressed state. I was at my wit's end, with a third person committing suicide, and the circumstances once again were "What could I have done differently?" I knew that the likelihood of knowing two people kill themselves was small, but to now have a third person was almost more than I could take. I had felt that Mitch was attracted to me, but there was nothing I could do about that. Julie was a friend and I would not go behind her back and cause her any pain or trouble in their relationship. I was hit with the guilt of this afterward. The questions kept running through my mind. "What if I had said something to Mitch? What if I had called Sam? What if I had spoken to my uncle? Would they still be alive?" What if? What if? What if?

After the hospitalization it became clear to me that it was time to draw back to God. I had never imagined that I'd get so far away from a life with Him in the first place. I started searching for a church again - one that I could call home and not just visit occasionally. Words cannot express how blessed I was to happen upon a Presbyterian church where the minister and his wife loved me enough that I truly felt welcome. In my wounded state, that was not something I felt very frequently. I even sang in the choir and every Sunday morning as we waited in line to sing the introit and process in, I would find myself paired with the minister's wife, Betty. One of my favorite introits became "What Does the Lord Require of You?" and it cited the scripture from Micah 6:8 - "To act justly, to love mercy and to walk humbly with your God." I would often think during Sunday morning service how blessed I was to be back in the house of God, and to sing on top of that! I was humbled to walk down that aisle every Sunday and be a part of God's family again. To be accepted by the minister and his wife, without feeling judged, was an added blessing. Betty was a delight, and she treated me just like everyone else, as did her husband Oluf. When I first joined the church they even offered to come visit me at my home. They had had an adventurous ministry being with "Up with People" and when I shared with them what I had been through, they started a support group for suicide survivors.

Unexpectedly though, Oluf had to have heart surgery and ultimately decided to retire. For me, I knew it marked the end of a very precious time in my life. A time where I had been nurtured and unconditionally loved, unlike the home I had grown up in. I knew more changes were coming in my own life, but I wasn't aware that God was about to turn the journey I was on into a bigger adventure than I could have ever planned.

Healing

The business I worked for had really slowed and there had been no new sales in almost a year. Darkness and depression seemed to be prevalent in my mind. I could not see a future in my life beyond the year 2000. This was very similar to the darkness that I sensed in my life when I was eighteen and could not see a life beyond it. I had never had those dreams of a wedding, husband and raising a family. I had always wondered to myself as a young girl, "Hmmm, I wonder what life will be like in the year 2000?" I had reached a benchmark of time in my mind and I wondered what on Earth my life was supposed to hold at that point. I was serving in the church but peace and healing still eluded me. Once again, the Lord was watching over me.

As I arrived at my desk early one Monday morning in July, I found myself in tears before I'd even turned the lights on. I had worked so hard at my career. I had sacrificed precious time with my son, in order to keep things running smoothly in my little corner of the company - going in between 6:30 a.m. and 7:00 a.m. and always working past five, with nothing more than a break to grab food and bring it back to my desk for lunch. My career helped my self-esteem and I was very good at what I did. I even traveled on business, giving presentations and training to clients whenever I could arrange it. I was considered one of the top consultants the company had, and to me it was proof positive that I had "recovered" completely from my debilitating anxiety. Still, when the work began to slack and business slowed, the plagues of depression and darkness that I couldn't understand began to return.

On that Monday morning, July 24, 2000, I heard a voice say "Just go, Mia." And I did. I decided to take a leave of absence from my job and try to find peace and resolution among the darkness inside. I literally put my life back in the Lord's hands by taking this leap of faith. I knew that because of my years of service I was eligible for the longest amount of personal leave that was allowed. My doctor and I consulted about whether I should go back into the hospital or not. We tried adjusting my medicine in all sorts of different combinations to find something that would work. Nothing did. Sure, I had a chemical imbalance that caffeine and any type of sugar could trigger, but the healing in my chemistry that I needed was emotional. Finally, in frustration with the roller coaster ride I was on, I said to myself, "Forget this stuff. It isn't helping," and I kicked all the medication at once. I was determined to "change my mind" and drive out the darkness that had plagued me for so long. And I would do it without prescription drugs.

I walked into my home that morning after leaving work, knowing that God was back once again on the throne of my life and I cried with relief, because I knew He was in control. It was hard giving up the career I had worked so diligently for, not knowing if I would ever go back again, but I knew it was the right thing to do. I felt God's precious presence with me that day as I turned my life back over to him and said "Okay, Lord, here's my life again. Your Will be done, not mine." God had finally set in motion the path to healing that I'd been searching subconsciously for, for so long.

Less than two weeks later, twenty eight people from my company were laid off. God had once again protected me. I was told I was not one of those being laid off, but there were murmurings to the contrary from other people. So there I was, unsure if I really had a job anymore or not. Instead of being thrown into panic and anxiety, the Lord protected me from fear. Every time I started to go down that familiar path of paranoid thinking and fear, He stopped it and reassured my mind. I just continued to live as if I had a job to go back to, and to seek the healing that I knew I had to have. Without it, I knew I couldn't go on. Something had to change.

One late summer day, about a month later, I heard an ad on the radio for a program on anxiety and depression. I really considered my anxiety at that point to be minimal and not a major issue. I mean, I had traveled and spoken in front of groups for work - I was cured, right? But the *peace* I longed for still eluded me, so I ordered the program. The information was really just for anxiety management and didn't go to the root of the problem, but it did help get me to the next phase of my recovery. It was a stepping stone that helped me to start to dig away at the layers of pain and rejection that had been buried in my subconscious for so long. I knew I would not find healing until I reached the core source of the pain and sadness that had begun so early in my life. I knew that a few prayers and claiming Isaiah 53:5 as my own, was not going to be enough. I was on a search for healing and freedom from the grief that wracked my soul so bitterly and I would not give up until I found it. I was done with pain and sadness; I was done with guilt and self-hatred. I was in the process of trading my sorrow in for the joy of the Lord. Jesus had set the path out before me and was covering me with His divine protection more than I even understood.

Because of our minister's retirement I was searching for a new church and the Lord led me to a bible based church which I had visited many years earlier, on what turned out to be Sanctity of Human Life Sunday in 2001. I didn't know what I was in for! In fact, if I'd known, I may not have ever made it there that Sunday. But praise God that I did.

The pastor talked about how his mother had been advised to abort him when he was in the womb. I sat in shock as tears rolled from this man's eyes and he pleaded with anyone who'd been through abortion or anyone who was willing to help, to get involved or seek healing. I realized for the first time that I was not alone in my pain that the lie of abortion had caused in my life. The pastor urged us to call one of the local crisis pregnancy centers and I did.

I'll never forget the day I went and met with Ann at a Christian based pro-life organization. When I explained to her how I'd been brought to her organization she said, "Well you must be here by divine appointment then!" I had little expectation other than I wanted to help other women in a crisis pregnancy make the same mistake I had. About an hour later, much to my surprise Ann knew not only about my abortion, but the agoraphobia, the suicides and the journey I'd been on. Ann thought I needed to find further healing before I could really help others. She encouraged me to take a twenty-six week course called Family Life Skills, which I did. It was kind of stressful initially, for me to go through the weekly "check-in," where each of us talked about what was going on in our lives. I wasn't used to having anyone listen to me as I grew up, so this was a new phenomenon for me! I had always shied away from the spotlight because of my family dynamic of being ignored; yet, I grew more and more comfortable as the weeks went on.

Finally in June of 2001, "it was time," as Ann put it. The next step on my journey of healing was to turn back to God's word in a deeper way, through a post-abortion Bible study. I needed to understand that I was forgiven. I can tell you quite honestly and simply that it was not easy, because I had believed the lie - that the baby was just tissue - not a real human being. In fact, it was one of the most painful things I have ever healed from. I feel that's why the Lord has impressed upon me the need to relate this story so strongly; if I can prevent this trauma from happening to any other young girls, and save unborn babies, my pain will be worth it. Perhaps they will never have to write words such as these, that I wrote to my baby for her memorial service:

My dearest Shantel,

The ache inside me is indescribable. Part of my soul died along with you on that day in September over twenty years ago. Somehow in my dreams I've managed to give birth to you instead of denying you, as I have for so many years. I see images of you and all the things I missed out on. I'll never get to hold you here on this Earth. I won't get to feed you, bathe you, cuddle and play with you or dress you in little girl clothes. I won't get to help you take your first steps or hear those first words from your lips. I won't be sending you off to kindergarten or dance lessons or high school or to college. Today you would be all grown up, a young lady and I know I love you now just as I would have if I'd had the wisdom and courage to keep you.

Love,

Mommy

After years and years of severe anxiety and many more of latent panic symptoms due to my abortion, God's love didn't just permeate my being with the flick of a light switch. It would take months and months for me to dig down deep and replace all the other lies that I had been told as a young girl, with God's Truth.

There was the lie that I would never be loved; that I was not worthy of love. I believed the lies that I had nothing important to say and I should keep quiet and not speak up, that I was not worth listening to and I would never amount to anything.

It took many months, but the Lord finally broke me of my unforgiveness toward myself and the sin of abortion. I had mourned the loss of my baby and I had released her to God, but I had never truly believed in my own heart that God could forgive me of such a terrible thing.

When He finally opened my eyes to His truth, once again, the floodgates of healing were released. As I placed this too, under the blood of Jesus, I became healthier than I'd ever been in my whole life. I know I can never repay what you've done for me Jesus. So, I'll share this story and let your Spirit do the rest. It's all about you Lord anyway, and what You desire for us is freedom - freedom through forgiveness and knowledge of You.

Afterword

Being named Meredith after my grandfather could have been my divine saving grace. During this journey of healing that the Lord has taken me on, it was revealed to me after a service at church one night, that my grandfather had sat me on his lap as a small child and prayed a prayer of purity for me. A few weeks after this, my grandfather appeared to me in a dream. I know he's in heaven because his glasses were shiny and gold rimmed, unlike the ones he wore here on earth. All I could see was his face, surrounded by white light. When I realized who it was, I gave him a kiss and his eyes opened up wide and his face lit up. At that point I woke up crying, realizing for the first time how much a simple little kiss meant to him.

I have a greater understanding now, of how one small gesture can mean so much to someone, especially the elderly. He was a charismatic man - proud, strong and yet after he broke his hip, he accepted his immobility very graciously. His presence and spirit filled a room, even if he could only sit humbly in his chair. When we would visit, all he wanted from me was a simple kiss that I was never too willing to share. I know he's watching over me. Somehow I know that Grandpa had prayed for me, and I thank God he did. The power of his prayer is what I believe helped sustain me through the darkest of days.

March 8, 2004

As my healing has progressed, God has used my greatest fear - that of public speaking - and turned it into His victory. Since January 2003, I have been speaking out about my abortion experience on behalf of Silent No More. On this night, I was asked to speak to the Students for Life at Iowa State University. What happened that night, I will never forget.

It had been almost twenty-one years, to the day, since Sam's suicide and in some ways it was at times, like a wound that had never completely healed. As I followed the directions I'd been given to the student union, I was amazed that the route I was taking was the same as I had taken on the night of March 11, 1983. Even though Sam was dead, I had had tickets to a concert at Hilton Coliseum on that night to see Diana Ross. I pondered whether to even attend or not, but the tickets were paid for and staying home wasn't going to bring Sam back, so I had decided to go. As I drove past the coliseum years later, the memories of that night began to come back to me.

I arrived at the union and during one of the speeches that night, the tumblers finally clicked into place and suddenly, I realized something very significant that had escaped me until that moment. Sam had been the father of an aborted baby during high school. All of a sudden the grief I had had for him made much more sense. Sam had been raised Catholic, and I remembered one Easter weekend he had gone to the nearest Catholic church off campus and talked to a priest. He had struggled with his role in abortion and was searching for forgiveness. As I thought back on this I realized, this was an important piece to the puzzle that led to his final fate. It was a sad realization, but it also brought more closure to one of the toughest things in life I've had to recover from. I pray that I see Sam in heaven one day.

November 3, 2013

Well Lord, I have come full circle, for sure. My story has remained untold, and today, of all days . . . . . thirty-five years after my very first journal entry, the day of my first kiss, You would prompt me to "finish this." You are simply amazing. I am in awe.

If you have had an abortion and this story has touched you with regret of your own.... I urge you to find healing and forgiveness as I did. There are several good Bible studies on post abortion out there. Look for a local crisis pregnancy center that has resources available for you to find peace. If you want to speak out - speak! Lastly, if you want to take a spiritual retreat, I recommend Rachel's Vineyard. The spiritual exercises and the structure of the weekend are fulfilling and monumental in providing the groundwork to a healthy self-esteem.

As I read back over this story, I feel like I'm a different person. Like all that grief, pain and unhappiness was someone else, in a way. I've come so far. Thank you for it all, Lord. Thank you that I never attempted to take my own life, although at times, it seemed inevitable. Thank you: for the tears, the joys, the hardships, and the challenges. When I spoke with a publisher regarding my story, she gave me the greatest of compliments that I will never forget. She said "You sound so healthy." And I know I am. What a victory! It was always my life's goal to feel healthy, and for the most part, I believe I've reached it! I know your love for me is real, Lord. Although it is hard at times to look back and reflect on the losses, you have made me stronger, more grateful and more humble with every breath of life. To God be the Glory, Amen.

Resources

Arin - Abortion Recovery International
www.abortionrecoveryinternational.org

Attacking Anxiety and Depression program
www.stresscenter.com

Care-Net
www.care-net.org

Forgiven and Set Free - A Post-Abortion Bible Study for Women by
Linda Cochrane

*Her Choice to Heal - Finding Spiritual and Emotional Peace After
Abortion*
by Sydna Masse
www.ramahinternational.org

NIMH – National Institute on Mental Health (Anxiety help)
www.nimh.nih.gov

Rachel's Vineyard Ministries
www.rachelsvineyard.org

Silent No More
www.silentnomoreawareness.org

Printed in the United States
By Bookmasters